CORAL REEFS

SEYMOUR SIMON

HARPER

An Imprint of HarperCollins*Publishers*

Special thanks to Randi Rotjan, Ph.D., Associate Scientist, New England Aquarium

PHOTO CREDITS: page 2: © Matthew Oldfield, Scubazoo/Photo Researchers, Inc.; page 3: © Reinhard Dirscherl/Visuals Unlimited, Inc.; pages 4–5: © Matthew Oldfield/Photo Researchers, Inc.; page 6: © Peter Scoones/Photo Researchers, Inc.; page 7: © Matthew Oldfield/Photo Researchers, Inc.; page 8: © Reinhard Dirscherl/Visuals Unlimited, Inc.; page 9, left to right: © Gregory Ochocki/Photo Researchers, Inc.; © Nancy Sefton/Photo Researchers, Inc.; © Andrew J. Martinez/Photo Researchers, Inc.; page 10, left to right: © Matthew Oldfield, Scubazoo/Photo Researchers, Inc.; © Georgette Douwma/Photo Researchers, Inc.; © Michael McCoy/Photo Researchers, Inc.; page 11: © Michael McCoy/Photo Researchers, Inc.; pages 12–13: © Matthew Oldfield, Scubazoo/Photo Researchers, Inc.; page 15: © Alexis Rosenfeld/Photo Researchers, Inc.; page 16: © John Maraventano/Photo Researchers, Inc.; page 17: © Burt Jones & Maurine Shimlock/Photo Researchers, Inc.; page 18: © Fred McConnaughey/Photo Researchers, Inc.; page 19, top: © Clay Coleman/Photo Researchers, Inc.; bottom: © Jeff Rotman/Photo Researchers, Inc.; page 20: © Gregory Ochocki/Photo Researchers, Inc.; page 21: © Anthony Bannister/Photo Researchers, Inc.; page 22: © Matthew Oldfield, Scubazoo/Photo Researchers, Inc.; page 23: © Matthew Oldfield/Photo Researchers, Inc.; pages 24–25: © David Fleetham/Visuals Unlimited, Inc.; page 27: © Tom & Therisa Stack/Photo Researchers, Inc.; pages 28–29: © Novastock/Photo Researchers, Inc.; pages 30–31: © Matthew Oldfield/Photo Researchers, Inc.

Library of Congress Cataloging-in-Publication Data
Simon, Seymour.
    Coral reefs / Seymour Simon. — 1st ed.
        p.   cm.
    ISBN 978-0-06-191495-9 (hardcover bdg.) — ISBN 978-0-06-191496-6 (pbk.)
    1. Coral reefs and islands—Juvenile literature.   2. Coral reef ecology—Juvenile literature.   I. Title.
GB461.S55   2013   2012019094
577.7'89—dc23   CIP
                                                                                                          AC

13   14   15   16   17   SCP   10 9 8 7 6 5 4 3 2 1
❖
First Edition

Dedicated with love to my wife, Liz,
helpmate with coral reefs and with life

Imagine diving beneath the waves into the warm waters of a tropical ocean. You're surrounded by strange rock shapes with brilliant colors: reds, greens, blues, oranges, and pinks. The colors change and shimmer and the waters are full of equally vibrant fish. There are other, strange-looking living things moving along the colorful rocks. This underwater world is like nothing you have ever seen on land. You are exploring a coral reef.

Coral reefs look like a bunch of rock formations. But a coral reef is actually a gigantic community of living things. For a long time, corals were a mystery to people. They were called rock-plants or plant-animals. Now we know that each coral polyp, basically a mouth, is a soft sea

animal that is something like a jellyfish. The polyp makes a hard, protective limestone skeleton.

Coral forms when a free-floating polyp attaches to a rock on a shallow seafloor of a tropical ocean. The polyp buds and divides again and again, developing into a large colony of thousands of mouths connected to one another.

As nearby colonies attach to each other, the framework of a coral reef forms. Coral reefs grow very slowly. In a hundred years, a coral colony may grow just a few feet. Coral reefs that began growing millions of years ago now stretch for hundreds of miles.

The two main kinds of coral are hard and soft. Reef-building corals are called hard corals because their skeletons are made of limestone. They usually have six tentacles, which help them catch food, tiny sea creatures called plankton. Algae, tiny green plants that shelter inside the polyps, use sunlight to make food for the coral. Hard corals are typically found in shallow waters less than one hundred feet deep. They are named for the way they look. Some common hard corals include table, elkhorn, branching, and brain corals; encrusting corals that look like mosses; and massive coral that looks like a rock boulder.

Table coral looks like a flat tabletop.

Branching coral has the appearance of a spiky tree with smaller branches reaching out.

Brain coral looks like the ridges of a brain.

Soft corals have different colors and shapes, such as fans, flowering plants, and folded pieces of leather. They usually have eight tentacles and feed only on plankton. They do not have stony skeletons and are not reef-building corals. They grow in both tropical seas and colder, deeper ocean waters, often bending and swaying in the ocean currents. You might typically find these corals in an aquarium.

Sea fans look like feathery fans growing on the sea bottom.

Sea whips branch into whiplike stalks.

Finger leather corals look like folded pieces of leather.

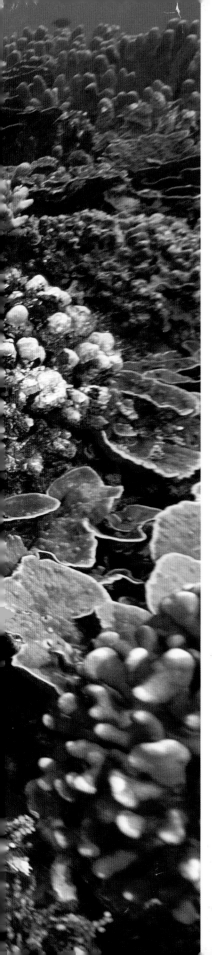

Most of the world's coral reefs are found in the warm waters of the Pacific Ocean, the Caribbean Sea, the Red Sea, the Arabian Gulf, and the Indian Ocean.

Coral reefs cover only a tiny fraction of the ocean floor, but they contain more than a quarter of all underwater ocean life. They are home to more than 4,000 kinds of fishes, 800 different kinds of hard coral, and many more thousands of other kinds of animals and plants. Scientists think that more than one million different species of animals and plants live in and around coral reefs.

There are three main kinds of coral reefs.

Fringing reefs are the most common kind of reef. They grow along the coastline around islands and continents. Between fringing reefs and the shore are narrow, shallow-water places called lagoons. When the tide is out, you can usually wade to shore from the reef. Fringing reefs often surround islands in the Caribbean Sea and in the South Pacific and Indian Oceans.

Barrier reefs also grow along a coastline but have deeper and wider lagoons separating them from the shore. The reefs form a barrier between the open sea and the lagoon. The Great Barrier Reef is the largest coral reef in the world, stretching for about 1,200 miles off the northeastern coast of Australia. Made of more than 2,500 smaller reefs strung together, it covers an area about the size of Kansas.

Coral atolls are rings of coral that surround large, deep central lagoons. More than 300 atolls are located in the South Pacific and Indian Oceans. A large atoll can be more than 100 miles across and surround lagoons of several thousand square miles.

A coral reef is like a city with many different kinds of citizens: fishes, crabs, clams, anemones, tube worms, algae, seaweed, and more. The reef provides shelter for thousands of fish species such as reef sharks, eels, parrotfish, angelfish, groupers, butterflyfish, pipefish, puffers, and rays. The fish have adaptations that help them find food or escape from becoming food.

Butterflyfish are brightly colored and boldly patterned reef fishes. The four-eyed butterflyfish has a large false eyespot at the base of its tail, similar to the eyespots on some butterfly wings. This may trick predators into attacking the wrong end, giving the butterflyfish a chance to escape.

Clownfish may be easy to spot, but by swimming among the stinging tentacles of a giant anemone, they can avoid becoming a meal for larger fish.

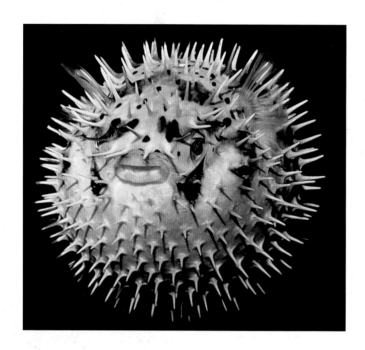

Porcupine fish are recognized by the sharp spikes that cover their heads and bodies. Larger fish usually won't attack them, but just in case they do, a porcupine fish quickly puffs up with seawater into a spiky ball at least double its original size.

A giant moray eel grows to more than six feet long. It hides within cracks and openings in a reef, perfectly blending in with the surrounding coral.

Colorful parrotfish use their chisel-like teeth to scrape coral for algae. While eating, the parrotfish grind the coral into the fine white sand found on tropical beaches.

A coral reef is also home to animals such as seabirds, porpoises, dolphins, manatees, sea turtles, sea snakes, and sharks. But invertebrates (animals without backbones), such as sponges, clams, and crabs, are the most common reef animals.

Sponges look like plants, but they are really animals. They attach themselves to hard pieces of coral skeleton and feed by drawing water into their bodies and filtering out plankton.

Sea stars and sea urchins have spiny skins. A giant adult sunflower sea star can be 3 feet across and have 16 to 24 arms. Each arm is studded with hundreds of tiny, powerful tube feet. Sea stars eat by turning their stomachs inside out (through their mouths) and surrounding and digesting the soft body of a clam, an urchin, a snail, or another sea star.

Clams, oysters, and snails are soft-bodied mollusks that usually have protective shells. Clams and oysters often lie buried in the sand or attach themselves to the hard coral. They eat by opening their shells and filtering plankton from the water. A clam can be as small as a thumbnail, or, like the giant clam of Australia's Great Barrier Reef, it can grow to more than 4 feet across and weigh over 500 pounds.

Some mollusks, such as the octopus, squid, and cuttlefish, don't have shells. The tiny, poisonous blue-ringed octopus lives in the deeper parts of Australian coral reefs.

Crabs, lobsters, and shrimp have hard, jointed outside skeletons. They hide in the cracks of the coral and crawl around the reef looking for food.

A coral reef at night is a living wall of tiny, tentacled mouths (polyps) feeding on plankton. Nighttime provides cover for many small reef animals from predators. It is also when the eggs of countless sea creatures hatch. Most plankton animals go on a daily elevator journey, rising to surface waters at nightfall and descending to the safety of deeper, darker waters at daybreak.

Nighttime reef fish look very different from daytime fish. They have dark colors and large eyes that reflect light. Some reef fishes that are colorful during the day even change to darker colors at night.

In many places around the world, coral reefs are threatened by water pollution, oil spills, and pesticides. They can be contaminated by construction along coasts, logging and farming along coastal rivers, and cutting down sea grasses and mangrove trees near the shore.

Another threat to coral reefs is a steady increase in average temperatures around the earth, called climate change or global warming. Most scientists think that the warming is caused by the greenhouse effect, an increase of carbon dioxide and other heat-trapping gases in our atmosphere. This causes ocean temperatures to rise, and as a result, some coral reefs are dying. Dying coral reefs are white or appear bleached.

Coral reefs are sometimes injured or destroyed when people mine the coral for building materials or break it to sell as souvenirs and jewelry. Sometimes tourist resorts build on reefs or empty sewage directly into a reef's surrounding waters. Dangerous fishing practices, such as fishing by using explosives, also harm reefs.

Millions of people depend upon coral reefs for their livelihoods. Small island countries with coral reefs rely on them to attract sightseers, scuba divers, snorkelers, and other tourists. They are an important source of food for the people who live nearby. Reefs in shore areas are shields from pounding waves, storm surges, and tsunamis.

Coral reefs are not just beautiful places to see and explore. Several important medical drugs for cancer research have been developed from chemicals found there.

People boast about building towering skyscrapers that compete for the title of being the biggest on the earth. But tiny animals can build coral reefs that are thousands of times larger than even the tallest skyscraper. No environment in nature is more colorful than a coral reef, and it is second only to a rainforest in the huge numbers of plants and animals that live there. Coral reefs may be out of our sight beneath the waves, but the beautiful images of coral will always be out of this world.

GLOSSARY

Algae—Simple green water plants without stems, leaves, or roots.

Anemone—Any of several invertebrate sea animals that are coelenterates, look like flowers, and have clusters of brightly colored tentacles around the mouth.

Atmosphere—A blanket of gases surrounding Earth or other planetary bodies that is held in place by gravitational forces.

Barrier reef—A coral reef roughly parallel to a shore and separated from it by a lagoon.

Carbon dioxide—A colorless, odorless gas formed when a carbon-based fuel is burned, when a human or animal exhales during respiration, or during photosynthesis in plants.

Coral polyp (also mouth)—A kind of small water animal attached at the bottom of its column-shaped body, with a mouth and small food-gathering tentacles at the other end. Polyps often grow in colonies and include corals, sea anemones, and hydras.

Global warming (also climate change)—A warming of Earth's atmosphere and oceans that is predicted to result from an increase in the greenhouse effect caused by an increase of carbon dioxide and other heat-trapping gases in our atmosphere.

Great Barrier Reef—The largest coral reef in the world, stretching for about 1,200 miles off the northeastern coast of Australia. Made of more than 2,500 smaller reefs strung together, it covers an area about the size of Kansas.

Greenhouse effect—A phenomenon that occurs when the sun's energy is trapped by Earth's atmosphere, producing temperatures that are warm enough to allow life to exist on Earth.

Lagoon—A shallow, saltwater lake either found within an atoll or separated from the sea by low-lying sandbanks. Also, a small freshwater lake or pond connected to a larger lake or river.

Plankton—Tiny animals and plants that live in the sea. Plankton plants float or drift in the water and are carried along by the currents.

INDEX